Eucharistic Participation

Eucharistic Participation

The Reconfiguration of Time and Space

Hans Boersma

REGENT COLLEGE PUBLISHING
Vancouver, British Columbia

Eucharistic Participation
Copyright © 2021 Hans Boersma

Regent College Publishing
5800 University Boulevard
Vancouver, BC V6T 2E4 Canada

All rights reserved. No part of this publication may be reproduced, stored in a retrieval system, or transmitted, in any form or by any means, electronic, mechanical, photocopying, recording or otherwise, without the prior written permission of the author, except in the case of brief quotations embodied in critical articles and reviews.

Regent College Publishing is an imprint of the Regent Bookstore (www.RegentBookstore.com). Views expressed in works published by Regent College Publishing are those of the author and do not necessarily represent the official position of Regent College (www.Regent-College.edu).

ISBN: 978-1-57383-593-0 (print)
ISBN: 978-1-57383-543-5 (ebook)

Contents

1. Eucharist and Time: Why Participation Means Sacrifice / 1

2. Eucharist and Place: Why Participation Means Real Presence / 37

1

Eucharist and Time: Why Participation Means Sacrifice

Polycarp's Eucharistic Sacrifice

The soldiers finally found him. They had pursued all the tricks in the book to find out where their victim was hiding. In the end, they had resorted to torture. One of the household slaves had finally cracked and given away the secret. Mounting their horses, the soldiers had scurried off to a little house, where in the Upper Room they found the person they had been looking for.[1] To their astonishment,

---

1. All info on Polycarp is taken from Alexander Roberts and James Donaldson, ed., *Ante-Nicene Fathers* (*ANF*), vol. 1 (1885, repr.; Peabody, Mass.: Hendrickson, 1994). *The Martyrdom of Polycarp* (*Mart Pol*) VII uses the term ὑπερῷον

the dangerous offender wasn't quite the robber type they had expected. Instead, he turned out to be an old man, hardly the kind of person that would seem to pose a danger to the empire. Nonetheless, orders were orders. And so it happened that around the year 155, the old Bishop Polycarp, at the age of 86, was dragged into the stadium of Smyrna, a town on the west coast of today's Turkey.

Face-to-face with the prospect of either lions or a burning stake, Polycarp did not cringe. In the eyewitness account, which we still have of *The Martyrdom of Polycarp*, we read what happened next: "[W]hen he came near, the proconsul asked him whether he was Polycarp. On his confessing that he was, [the proconsul] sought to persuade him to deny [Christ], saying, 'Have respect for your old age,' and other similar things, according to their custom, [such as], 'Swear by the fortune of Caesar; repent, and say, Away with the Atheists.'" (Christians, as you may know, were often called 'atheists' because they refused to worship the Roman gods.) What would Polycarp do?

> But Polycarp, gazing with a stern countenance on all the multitude of the wicked heathen then in the stadium, and waving his hand towards them, while

---

(upper room; *Patrologiæ Græcæ* [*PG*] 5.1033), which is also used in Acts 1:13; 9:37, 39; 20:8. The word ἀνώγεον is used in Mark 14:15 and Luke 22:12.

> with groans he looked up to heaven, said, "Away with the Atheists." Then, the proconsul urging him, and saying, "Swear, and I will set you free, reproach Christ;" Polycarp declared, "86 years have I served him, and he never did me any injury; how then can I blaspheme my King and my Saviour?"[2]

These famous words of Bishop Polycarp, spoken in the stadium of Smyrna, have echoed through the centuries of the history of the church. Shortly after these words, the soldiers tied his hands behind his back and led Polycarp to the stake, on which he offered his thanksgiving, his εὐχαριστία, to God, ending with the words, "I praise Thee for all things, I bless Thee, I glorify Thee, along with the everlasting and heavenly Jesus Christ, Thy beloved Son, with whom, to Thee, and the Holy Ghost, be glory both now and to all coming ages. Amen."[3] Those were the last words of St. Polycarp as he sacrificed his entire self in εὐχαριστία to his God and Saviour. Polycarp's words are the liturgical prayer spoken in preparation before he offers up his Eucharistic sacrifice.

Several close links connect this story of the martyrdom of Polycarp with the Gospel of John, and in particular with chapter 15, where Jesus says to his disciples, "I am the

2. *Mart Pol* IX (*ANF* 1.41).
3. *Mart Pol* XIV (*ANF* 1.42).

vine; you are the branches. Whoever abides in me and I in him, he it is that bears much fruit, for apart from me you can do nothing" (John 15:5).⁴ We read in *The Maryrdom of Polycarp* that the soldiers "found him lying down in the upper room (ἐν ὑπερῴῳ) of a certain little house."⁵ In John 15, Jesus and his disciples also find themselves in the "upper room." John 15, as you know, is the central chapter of Jesus' lengthy "Upper Room Discourse." Though we don't know where Polycarp got his name, it definitely was an appropriate one.⁶ Polycarp's name was a reminder—both to the Bishop himself and to his parishioners—that his purpose in life was to bear much fruit— πολὺς καρπός. Some time before he got martyred, St. Polycarp wrote a letter to the Philippians—the same people that also received a letter from the apostle Paul. At the very beginning of that letter, Polycarp makes quite clear that not only does he want to be a true "Polycarp" himself, but he also wants the

---

4. Throughout these two essays, I use the English Standard Version.

5. *Mart Pol* VII (*ANF* 1.40).

6. John Foster has suggested that Polycarp received his espiscopal name from St. John in the light of the challenge that these verses posed ("A Note on St. Polycarp," *Expository Times* 77 [1966]:319). Cf. Raymond E. Brown, *The Gospel according to John (xiii-xxi)*, The Anchor Bible, 29A (Garden City, NY: Doubleday, 1966), 661.

church to which he writes to be "polycarps." He writes to them: "I have greatly rejoiced with you in our Lord Jesus Christ, because ... the strong root of your faith ... persists even until now, and brings forth fruit to our Lord Jesus Christ, who for our sins suffered even unto death."[7] The reason for Polycarp's joy is that the root of the Philippians' faith has produced fruit. The Philippians themselves are apparently bearing much fruit, πολὺς καρπός. There is no greater joy for Bishop Polycarp than to see that his parishioners, too, are turning into "polycarps." Note the parallel with John 15: "Whoever abides in me and I in him, he it is that bears much fruit (καρπὸν πολύν)" (15:5). "By this my Father is glorified, that you bear much fruit (καρπὸν πολὺν) and so prove to be my disciples" (15:8).

In this essay, I will deal with the Eucharist. And in particular, I want to ask what it means to offer up everything we have received from God, in thanksgiving, in Eucharistic worship in the Upper Room. In other words, I will discuss what it means to be a "polycarp," to join the old Bishop in the Upper Room, and to offer up ourselves in sacrifice. One thing it clearly means is that we join not just Polycarp, but—since Polycarp is one of the branches of the vine—along with him also Jesus himself. Whether or not

---

7. *The Epistle of Polycarp to the Philippians* I, in ANF 1.33. *PG* 5.1005A uses the words ῥίζα (root) and καρποφορεῖ (bear fruit).

Polycarp intentionally conjures up for us the Upper Room Discourse of St. John's Gospel, I am not sure. Of course, he was one of John's direct disciples, and as such it would not have been out of place for him to have chosen as his episcopal identity a name that echoed Jesus' words of John 15. Nor would it have been out of place for the church of Smyrna—in relating the account of their beloved bishop's death—to have noted the remarkable fact that Polycarp, like Jesus, was in the Upper Room in the days immediately preceding his martyrdom. Regardless of what may or may not have been in the mind of the author, however, I am going to suggest that there is a deeper link that connects Polycarp to Jesus, and this has to do with the overall theology of John chapter 15, and indeed with the theology of the entire Gospel. "I am the vine," says Jesus; "you are the branches. Whoever abides in me and I in him, he it is that bears much fruit, for apart from me you can do nothing" (15:5). These simple words give us the deepest grounds why the life of Polycarp is patterned on that of Christ. Or, I should perhaps say: these words of Jesus give us the deepest grounds why the life of Polycarp *participates* in that of Christ. "I am the vine; you are the branches." These words bring us to the heart of Eucharistic doctrine and to the heart of our understanding of the church. The doctrine of the Eucharist and the church is all about participation in Christ. It is all about the branches being united to the vine, depending for their life and fruit upon the vine: "As the branch cannot bear fruit by itself, unless it abides in the vine, neither can you, unless you abide in me" (15:4).

The verb "abide" (μένω) is used ten times in this passage. We are clearly meant to take note: our bearing fruit depends on us as branches abiding in Christ as the vine. Nor is this participation something we do merely as individuals. "You brought a vine out of Egypt; you drove out the nations and planted it," sings Asaph in Psalm 80. "You cleared the ground for it; it took deep root and filled the land. The mountains were covered with its shade, the mighty cedars with its branches. It sent out its branches to the sea and its shoots to the River" (Ps 80:9-11). The Psalmist tells the story of the exodus from Egypt to the Promised Land, and he says it's like God taking a vine from one piece of land and transplanting it into another, moving it from Egypt to Canaan. Clearly, Israel is the vine. We cannot pursue this further here, but we find the same identification of Israel as the vine throughout the Old Testament.[8] There is even a passage in Jeremiah 2 that identifies Israel as the "true vine" (Jer 2:21). For Jesus to insist that he is the true vine is to say nothing less than that he is the true Israel. By abiding or participating in Christ, then, we are joining the true Israel. To join Christ and to

---

8. Cf. Hosea 10, Isaiah 5, Jeremiah 2, Ezekiel 15.

join the church are one and the same thing. The two are quite simply inseparable.

It is hardly a coincidence that it is on the occasion where he instituted the Eucharist—the celebration of the Last Supper—that Jesus is telling his disciples as well as us to abide in the vine. Polycarp, too, was undoubtedly aware that it is in the Upper Room, along with the Apostles (Acts 2:13), that one is united to Jesus, that one participates in him by eating the "living bread" (John 6:51) and by drinking the "fruit of the vine" (Mark 14:25; Matt 26:29). Jesus is both the living bread and the true vine (John 6:51; 15:1). "Greater love has no one than this, that someone lay down his life for his friends," comments Jesus as he explains the story of the vine and the branches (15:13). Jesus' identity as the true vine calls to mind his sacrificial love in dying the martyr's death for the sake of his friends. It is this same sacrificial love in which Polycarp participates when he, too, leaves the Upper Room to give his life for the church of Smyrna and also for us. And it is this same sacrificial love in which we participate when we share in the Eucharistic celebration. "Truly, truly, I say to you"—this is John 12:24—"unless a grain of wheat falls into the earth and dies, it remains alone; but if it dies, it bears much fruit (πολὺν καρπὸν φέρει)." The fruit-bearing of a "polycarp" has to do with participating in the sacrificial martyrdom of Jesus. The Lutheran New Testament scholar, Oscar Cullmann, helpfully observes: "The relation between the branch and the vine is, therefore, above all, the eucharistic communion of believers with Christ."[9] Whenever we celebrate the Eucharist, we become a "polycarpic" congregation by offering ourselves up, by participating in the very sacrifice of Christ.

---

9. Oscar Cullmann, *Early Christian Worship*, trans. A. Stewart Todd and James B. Torrance (London: SCM, 1966), 113. Quoted in Raymond E. Brown, *The Gospel according to John (xiii-xxi)*, The Anchor Bible, vol. 29A (Garden City, NY: Doubleday, 1966), 673-74. For Brown, Cullmann's claim is too far-reaching, since the relationship of believers with Christ is, in this passage, primarily one of love (and faith) and only secondarily Eucharistic. This may be true in terms of historical meaning, but theologically love and Eucharistic participation are inseparable. For further support of a Eucharistic reading, Brown points to the Eucharistic blessing of *Didache* 11:2 ("We thank you, our Father, for the holy vine of David your servant, which you revealed to us through Jesus your servant."), which is significant considering the similarity between the *Didache*'s words about the Eucharistic bread and John's account of the multiplication of the loaves (ibid., 673). Brown further alerts us to the similarity between 15:5 and 6:56; the overall passage and 6:57; 15:13 and 6:51. Comments Brown: "The 'I am the living bread' of vi 51 and 'I am the real vine' of xv 1 form a Johannine diptych not unlike 'This is my body' and 'This is my blood'" (ibid., 673).

Filling up Christ's Afflictions?

It seems to me that we see something of this participation in Christ's sacrifice in St. Paul's letter to the Colossians, when he writes in 1:24: "Now I rejoice in my sufferings for your sake, and in my flesh I am filling up what is lacking in Christ's afflictions for the sake of his body, that is, the church."[10] This is, in various ways, a puzzling passage. First, we have the remarkable fact that the Apostle claims to be rejoicing in suffering—something that certainly our culture would consider a rather odd claim. Second, for the Apostle to say that there are things that are lacking—τὰ ὑστερήματα in Greek—in Christ's afflictions would also seem out of place; it is almost as though he were denying the once-for-all sufficiency of Christ's sacrificial death. Doesn't he make it appear as though he exalts human merit, in the sense that we earn our own salvation—even if it is by means of suffering?

Of course, the notion that there is joy in suffering is not unique to Colossians 1:24. In many places, St. Paul ex-

---

10. The following reflections on Col 1:24 are taken from Hans Boersma, *Violence, Hospitality, and the Cross: Reappropriating the Atonement Tradition* (Grand Rapids: Baker Academic, 2004), 231-33.

presses his joy in the midst of suffering and boasts of it.[11] His reason for this joy does not lie in Paul's personal character, in his personal ability to put up with difficult circumstances. After all, with the right disposition we might *grin* and bear difficult things, but we would not *rejoice* in suffering. To grasp at least to some extent how Paul is able to write that he can rejoice in his sufferings, we need to move briefly into what forms a likely historical backdrop to his comment. Circumstances in the centuries before the birth of Christ had forced the Jewish people of God to reflect on their suffering—in particular the suffering of continuous oppression and domination. How could it be that while being faithful to the Torah, they were nonetheless oppressed by powers hostile to the kingdom of God? Why did God not have mercy on his people? In this situation, the Jewish people developed a martyrdom theology.[12] Without necessarily seeking out suffering, they began to realize that through suffering they were obtaining a place

---

11. E.g., Rom 5:3; 2 Cor 1:5-7; 4:1-18; 7:4; 11:23-27; Gal 6:17; 1 Thess 1:6. Cf. James D.G. Dunn, *The Epistles to the Colossians and to Philemon: A Commentary on the Greek Text*; New International Greek Testament Commentary (Grand Rapids: Eerdmans; Carlisle: Paternoster, 1996), 114.

12. Cf. John S. Pobee, *Persecution and Martyrdom in the Theology of Paul* (Sheffield: JSOT, 1985), 13-46.

in God's plan of redemption. We find this reflected in the Fourth Book of Maccabees:

> These then, having consecrated themselves for the sake of God, are now honored not only with this distinction but also by the fact that through them our enemies did not prevail against our nation, and the tyrant was punished and our land purified, since they became, as it were, a ransom for the sin of our nation. Through the blood of these righteous ones and through the propitiation of their death the divine providence rescued Israel, which had been shamefully treated [4 Macc 17:20-22].[13]

The Jewish martyrs came to regard themselves not just as enduring foreign oppression by way of punishment from God or as suffering injustice inflicted on them by their enemies, but as participating in the redemption of God's people.[14]

---

13. Translations of 4 Maccabees are taken from James H. Charlesworth, ed., *The Old Testament Pseudepigrapha*, vol. 2 (Garden City, NY: Doubleday, 1985).

14. For more extensive elaborations of this theme in intertestamental literature, see N.T. Wright, *The New Testament and the People of God*, vol. 1 of *Christian Origins and the Question of God* (Minneapolis, Minn.: Fortress, 1992), 276-79; *Jesus and the Victory of God*, vol. 2 of *Christian Origins* (Minneapolis, Minn.: Fortress, 1996), 577-84. Cf. Manfred T. Brauch, *Hard*

Especially since Albert Schweitzer's 1906 publication on the historical Jesus, New Testament scholars have often pointed out the significance of this suffering of the so-called "messianic woes," which are the birth pangs of the new age of the Kingdom of God.[15] They constitute a time of concentrated, redemptive suffering of certain individuals on behalf of the entire nation so as to give birth to the messianic age. Without this suffering, the dawning of the new age would be impossible, because God would continue to be angry with his people. And so the martyrs prayed, "Be merciful to your people and let our punishment be a satisfaction on their behalf. Make my blood their purification and take my life as a ransom for theirs" (4 Macc 6:27-29).

The early Jewish Christians interpreted Christ's messianic suffering in the light of this overall picture of the "messianic woes" that would introduce the new age of

---

Sayings of Paul (Downers Grove, Ill.: InterVarsity, 1989), 234-39; Leonardo Boff, *Passion of Christ, Passion of the World: The facts, their Interpretation, and Their Meaning Yesterday and Today*, trans. Robert R. Barr (Maryknoll, NY: Orbis, 1987), 60, 75-78.

15. Albert Schweitzer, *The Quest for the Historical Jesus: A Critical Study of Its Progress from Reimarus to Wrede*, trans. W. Montgomery, 3rd ed. (London: Black, 1954), 385-86. Cf. Pobee, *Persecution*, 38-39; Wright, *Jesus*, 578.

the resurrection. The "afflictions" of Christ that Paul mentions in Colossians need to be understood, suggests Peter O'Brien in his commentary, against "the OT and Jewish background with its apocalyptic conception of the afflictions of the end time, the woes of the Messiah."[16] When St. Paul comments that he rejoices that in his flesh he is filling up what is lacking in Christ's afflictions, his joy stems not from the sufferings in themselves, but from the fact he is allowed to share in the messianic suffering of Christ. James D. G. Dunn rightly comments:

> The claim is not megalomaniac.... It is rather the most striking expression of a conviction which Paul seems to have had from the beginning of his apostolic ministry, namely that his mission was to fulfill or complete that of the Servant of Yahweh, that is, also of the suffering Servant of deutero-Isaiah. This underlines in turn the degree to which Paul understood his apostleship in eschatological terms as the last act on the stage of this world before (as we would say) the final curtain (particularly 1 Cor. 4:9). It was because Paul saw himself as a major actor in the final drama of God's reconciling purpose that he could also see his all too real sufferings as somehow bringing to completion what was still outstanding of the sufferings of Christ ("crucified

---

16. Peter T. O'Brien, *Colossians, Philemon*; Word Biblical Commentary, 44 (Waco, Tex.: Word, 1982), 78.

with Christ") by which the world was redeemed and transformed.[17]

The Pauline notion of Christians being crucified with Christ is not an abstract theological idea, but gives rise to his joyful willingness to suffer to the point of sacrificial martyrdom in and with Christ.

This, it seems to me, explains why Polycarp patterns his actions on those of Christ in the Upper Room. He is participating in the very sufferings of Christ, filling up what is still lacking in Christ's afflictions. Indeed, in his book, *Cruciformity: Paul's Narrative Spirituality of the Cross*, Michael J. Gorman insists that this pattern of cruciformity reaches beyond St. Paul to all Christian believers. The metanarrative of Pauline theology is, he writes, "an ongoing pattern of living in Christ and of dying with him that produces a Christ-like (cruciform) person. Cruciform existence is what being Christ's servant, indwelling him and being indwelt by him, living with and for and 'according to' him, is all about, for individuals and communities."[18] For Gorman, this implies that cruciform suffering is an integral part of the life of the Christian community.

---

17. Dunn, *Colossians and Philemon*, 116-17.
18. Michael J. Gorman, *Cruciformity: Paul's Narrative Spirituality of the Cross* (Grand Rapids: Eerdmans, 2001), 49.

This cruciformity is more than mere imitation of Christ: "Cruciformity misunderstood as the human imitation of Christ is indeed an impossibility. However, cruciformity is the initial and ongoing work of Christ himself—by his Spirit sent by God—who dwells within each believer and believing community, shaping them to carry on the story (Phil 4:13)."[19]

This last point is crucial. According to Gorman, our cruciform lives are not separate from the cruciform life of Christ. In some mysterious way, our self-sacrifice is a participation in the sacrifice of Christ. If we view the sacrifices that we offer as separate from that of Christ, we end up with two distinct kinds of sacrifices—the one offered by Christ, the others by us. That would lead to all sorts of problems, not the least of which is the question I raised earlier: wouldn't this be a denial of the sufficiency of the sacrifice of Christ? How could we add a second sacrifice to the once-for-all (ἐφάπαξ) character of Christ's sacrifice that the letter to the Hebrews insists upon (Heb 7:27; 9:12, 26; 10:10)? Furthermore, if we separate our sacrifices from his, we need to realize that the implication is that Christ himself offers only the one sacrifice, namely, his own; and that therefore the other sacrifices are those that *we* offer, on our own, by ourselves. It's hard to avoid a Pelagian,

---

19. Ibid., 400.

pull-yourself-up-by-your-own-bootstraps theology if we are left to offer the second type of sacrifice—our own—by ourselves.[20]

And yet, it's impossible to get around the notion that the Lord does call on us to offer sacrifices. We are "like living stones [that] are being built up as a spiritual house, to be a holy priesthood, to offer spiritual sacrifices acceptable to God through Jesus Christ" (1 Pet 2:5). The Apostle appeals to us in Romans 12:1 to "present [our] bodies as a living sacrifice, holy and acceptable to God, which is your spiritual worship." Paul explains to the Philippians—perhaps the most joyful book in all of Scripture: "Even if I am to be poured out as a drink offering upon the sacrificial offering of your faith, I am glad and rejoice with you all" (Phil 2:17). Sacrifice is a Christian calling, and—as this last verse from Philippians makes clear and as we have seen from our reflections on Colossians 1:24—this sacrifice may in the end involve martyrdom. Sacrifice is part and

---

20. Cf. Thomas F. Torrance's comment: "Thus, if the human priesthood of Jesus Christ is set within a damaging dualist context ... we are thrown back upon ourselves to effect our own 'Pelagian' mediation with God by being our own priests and by offering to him our own sacrifices" ("The Paschal Mystery of Christ and the Eucharist," in *Theology in Reconciliation: Essays towards Evangelical and Catholic Unity in East and West* [Grand Rapids: Eerdmans, 1975], 106-38, at 133-34).

parcel of the Christian life. The reason why none of these sacrifices add a new, second sacrifice to that of Christ, and the reason why we don't offer them up on our own strength, is that there really is only one sacrifice, namely, that of Christ—and the sacrifices that we offer up merely *participate* in that one sacrifice of Christ.

I suspect that one reason why so many of our churches have done away with a sacramental view of the Eucharist is that people are nervous about the notion that we would offer something to God in the Eucharist. And, frankly, that's not a bad nervousness to have. If indeed we have two distinct sacrifices—the one on Golgotha and the other one in church—then we have a serious problem. That is something the Reformers rightly were apprehensive about. Martin Luther, for instance, claimed: "We know and have no other sacrifice than that which [Christ] made on the cross on which he died once for all."[21] "Christ has sacrificed himself once; henceforth he will not be sacrificed by anyone else."[22] And John Calvin asked rhetorically, "Are we allowed daily to sew innumerable patches upon such a sacrifice [i.e., that of Christ], as if it were im-

---

21. *Luther's Works*, vol. 36, p. 313. Quoted in George Hunsinger, *The Eucharist and Ecumenism* (Cambridge: Cambridge University Press, 2008), 101.

22. *Luther's Works*, vol. 36, p. 147. Quoted in Hunsinger, *Eucharist and Ecumenism*, 101.

perfect, when he has so clearly commended its perfection? When God's Sacred Word not only affirms but cries out and contends that this sacrifice was performed only once and all its force remains forever, do not those who require another sacrifice accuse it of imperfection and weakness?"[23] These objections seem to me entirely right—at least, when directed against the notion that there are two separate sacrifices, one offered by Christ and another that we offer ourselves. And, unfortunately, there is a great deal to suggest that this is exactly the way people often looked at the Eucharistic sacrifice in the late Middle Ages, which made the Reformation reaction quite understandable.[24]

From Univocal Time to Sacramental Time

But we need to ask: is this notion of what Christ offers up and what we offer up being two different sacrifices the only way of looking at things? I am going to suggest that, no, it is not. But to be able to see this is going to require

---

23. John Calvin, *Institutes of the Christian Religion*, ed. John T. McNeill, trans. Ford Lewis Battles, vol. 2 (Philadelphia, Penn.: Westminster Press, 1960), IV.xviii.3.

24. Gregory Dix, *The Shape of the Liturgy* (Westminster: Dacre, 1945), 623; J. M. R. Tillard, "Sacrificial Terminology and the Eucharist," *One in Christ* 17 (1981): 306-21, at 319. Cf. Hunsinger, *Eucharist and Ecumenism*, 125-26.

some work, since the modern age has made it difficult for us to see that the same sacrifice that was offered up 2,000 years ago can somehow be sacrificed also today.[25] We tend to look at time as a simple succession of distinct moments, unrelated to one another; we regard event "X," which took place 2,000 years ago, as no longer present, and thus in principle as unconnected to event "Y," which is taking place today. This is not to say that we deny historical cause and effect. We realize quite well that through a number of traceable historical causes, event "X" gives rise to event "Y." As Charles Taylor puts it in his book, *A Secular Age*: "We have constructed an environment in which we live a uniform, univocal secular time, which we try to measure and control in order to get things done."[26] When Taylor talks about "univocal" time, what he means is a view of time in which the one hour is no different from the next (*unus* meaning "one"; *vox* meaning "voice"; so, we speak in "one voice"), in which *chronos* gets the dull sense of inevitability, of inexorably marching on, seeing that God's action in no way impacts history. As a result, univocal

---

25. The following two paragraphs follow closely my book, *Heavenly Participation: The Weaving of a Sacramental Tapestry* (Grand Rapids: Eerdmans, 2011), 125-27.

26. Charles Taylor, *A Secular Age* (Cambridge, Mass.: Belknap – Harvard University Press, 2007), 59.

time gives us the control that we crave in the secularity of modernity.

St. Augustine, in Book XI of his *Confessions*, makes clear that as far as he is concerned, past, present, and future are not simply successive moments of secular or univocal time. His sacramental mindset opens Augustine to the realization that "it is inexact language to speak of three times—past, present, and future."[27] The reason is that for St. Augustine, these three co-exist in the human mind and, even more importantly, are identical in the eternity of God himself. St. Augustine's concept of time is sacramental: time *participates* in the eternity of God's life, and it is this participation that is able to gather past, present, and future together into one.[28] Charles Taylor illustrates this point by referring to the two events of the sacrifice of Isaac and the Crucifixion of Christ. You will recall Abraham's comment in the narrative of the Binding of Isaac, after Isaac had asked his father, "Behold, the fire and the wood, but where is the lamb for a burnt offering?" (Gen 22:7). Abraham's response was, "God will provide for himself the lamb for a burnt offering, my son" (Gen 22:8). Charles Taylor points out that for the pre-modern Christian, the

---

27. St. Augustine, *Confessions*, trans. Henry Chadwick (Oxford: Oxford University Press, 1991), 235 (XI.20)

28. I am drawing on Taylor's distinction between "Plato eternity" and "God's eternity" (*Secular Age*, 57).

Binding of Isaac and the Crucifixion were linked together, that the former participated in the latter: "These two events were linked through their immediate contiguous places in the divine plan. They are drawn close to identity in eternity, even though they are centuries (that is, 'aeons' or 'saecula') apart. In God's time there is a sort of simultaneity of sacrifice and Crucifixion."[29] The Binding of Isaac, you could say, was a sacrament of the Crucifixion. What that means is that the former participates in the latter. The Augustinian view of time—and that is key here—allows for the participation of one historical event in another. The sacrifice of Isaac and the Crucifixion of Christ are not simply two univocal and separate events; rather, the sacrifice of Isaac participates in the Crucifixion of Christ, just as the sign of a sacrament participates in its reality.

The example of the Binding of Isaac and the Crucifixion of Christ is not just a random one. It alludes to the fact that it is in Christ that ordinary or successive time participates most fully and gloriously in the eternity of God. Christ himself, we could say, is *the* great sacrament, the mystery par excellence. In him, the eternal Word has entered into the temporal succession of events, thus allowing time to participate sacramentally in eternity. Through the Incarnation, you could also say, the separa-

---

29. Ibid., 55.

tion between heaven and earth has been broken down. Every temporal event that takes place in the ordinary time of human history thus derives its being and significance from the great Christ event. Temporal events have meaning and value because of their participation in, their sacramental connection to—or their "simultaneity" with, as Taylor calls it—the Incarnate Word, Jesus Christ himself.

The Reformed ecumenical scholar, George Hunsinger, applies this notion—that in Christ time itself begins to participate in eternity—to our sacrificial understanding of the Eucharist. Rightly warning against language of "re-enactment" and "repetition" in connection with what happens at the Eucharist,[30] Hunsinger has a clear eye for the truth element in the objections of the Reformers. We cannot have multiple sacrifices without endangering the once-for-all character of Christ's sacrifice and lapsing into the heretical notion that in the Eucharist we offer up what are strictly our own works, things that we have accomplished in our own strength.[31] Hunsinger,

---

30. Hunsinger, *Eucharist and Ecumenism*, 172.

31. Cf. St. John Chrysostom's comment in his *Homilies on Hebrews*, in Philip Schaff, ed., *Nicene and Post-Nicene Fathers*, vol. I/14 (1889, repr.; Peabody, Mass., 1994), XVII.6 (449): "What then? do not we offer every day? We offer indeed, but making a remembrance of His death, and this [remembrance] is one and not many. How is it one, and not many? Inasmuch as

however, suggests that the notion of participation is able to overcome this problem of two different sacrifices. If our sacrifice participates in that of Christ, then it is simply another way of saying what St. Paul himself says in Colossians 1:24, namely, that we fill up what is "lacking"—between quotation marks—in Christ's afflictions. This filling up is nothing but a participation in the one, unique sacrifice offered by Christ on the Cross, something that in turn is possible because time is not just a chronological succession of distinct moments but is held together in and by Christ. The sacrifice of Isaac, the sacrifice of Christ on the Cross, and our sacrifice in church are not three distinct sacrifices; they are one and the same. Hunsinger puts it this way:

> [E]ucharistic sacrifice involves three tenses of salvation. It is not another sacrifice than the sacrifice of the cross. It is rather the same sacrifice in sacramental form. It is the form that occurs in the time between the times—in the time between Calvary and the Messianic Banquet. The eucharistic sacrifice is therefore at once provisional and anticipato-

---

that [Sacrifice] was once for all offered, [and] carried into the Holy of Holies. This is a figure of that [sacrifice] and this remembrance of that. For we always offer the same, not one sheep now and to-morrow another, but always the same thing: so that the sacrifice is one" (square brackets in original).

ry, a matter of *anamnesis* [remembrance] but also of *prolepsis* [anticipation]. It is salvation's occurrence in the present tense. It actualizes, mediates, and attests the *Christus praesens* [present Christ] in the past and future forms of his royal and priestly offices.... *Anamnesis* [remembrance], intercession, and *prolepsis* [anticipation] all converge in the eucharistic sacrifice. They converge through the prayer of *epiclesis* [invocation]. The invocation of the Holy Spirit brings the past and future into the present. Eternity is made present to time, and time to eternity, as well.[32]

On Hunsinger's understanding, there is nothing magical or automatic about this. Past, present, and future converge only when God's Spirit *makes* them converge. Our sacrifices enter into Christ's—our martyrdom enters into that of Christ—only as the result of the Spirit listening to our prayers. It is the power of the Spirit that allows our sacrifices to participate in that of Christ.

What is more, Hunsinger also recognizes—and here he appeals to T. F. Torrance—that talk of Eucharistic sacrifice should never assume that the Cross and the Eucharist are of equal weight. The three events—the Binding of Isaac, the Crucifixion, and the Eucharist—all have a sacrificial character. But the first and the last have their mean-

---

32. Ibid., 177.

ing always only in radical dependence on the second. Put differently, the Binding of Isaac and the Eucharist participate in the sacrifice of Christ, not the other way around. (The sacrifice of Christ does not participate in the Binding of Isaac or in the Eucharist.) Hunsinger puts it this way:

> The cross is always central, constitutive, and definitive, while the eucharist is always secondary, relative, and derivative.... The cross was styled by Torrance as the "dimension of depth" in the eucharist. The eucharist has no significance in itself that is not derived from the cross and grounded in it. Therefore the cross alone is the saving "content, reality and power" of the eucharist. It is a matter of one reality, one priestly sacrifice of Christ, in two different temporal forms.[33]

Notice how, again, Hunsinger insists on the one sacrifice being present in two different forms—the form of the Cross and the form of the Eucharist. But he rightly notes that the two are not simply exchangeable. The Eucharistic sacrifice is a sacrifice because it participates in the priestly sacrifice on the Cross, and it does so only

---

33. Hunsinger, *Eucharist and Ecumenism*, 151. Cf. idem, "The Dimension of Depth: Thomas F. Torrance on the Sacraments of Baptism and the Lord's Supper," *Scottish Journal of Theology* 54 (2001): 155-76. Hunsinger also appeals to Torrance, *Theology in Reconciliation*, 82.

because of the gracious and powerful working of the Holy Spirit. There is no Eucharistic sacrifice without *epiklēsis*, without invocation of the Spirit.

Why Participation Implies Sacrifice

There is one final question that I want to address. What I have mostly done is to try and make it plausible for us to look at the communion meal through a sacrificial lens. I have done this by appealing to the notion of "participation." "I am the vine; you are the branches. Whoever abides in me and I in him, he it is that bears much fruit" (John 15:5). It is our participation in the vine that allows us to speak of Christian martyrdom, and that allowed Polycarp to speak of his life and ours as bearing much fruit. "Now I rejoice in my sufferings for your sake, and in my flesh I am filling up what is lacking in Christ's afflictions for the sake of his body, that is, the church" (Col 1:24). It is our participation in the once-for-all sacrifice of Christ that allows us to rejoice as we share in this unique sacrifice of Christ on the Cross. "God will provide for himself the lamb for a burnt offering, my son" (Gen 22:8). It is the participation of our chronological time in eternity, by means of the Christ event, that makes it plausible for us to say that both the Binding of Isaac and the Eucharist participate in the once-for-all sacrifice of Christ.

Eucharistic Participation

Still, to be plausible is not the same as to be actually so. In other words, yes, we may operate with a biblical notion of "union with Christ" or of "participation in Christ"; and yes, that may require us to reconfigure our understanding of time itself—but why would that compel us to speak of the Eucharist in sacrificial terms? Why does participation imply sacrifice? There are two reasons for this. The one reason—the most basic—has really been implicit in everything I have argued so far. But I should draw it out and make it explicit. There are broadly two approaches to the way we understand the Eucharist. The one is participatory, the other non-participatory. Of course, as a result of the Reformation, we have more than just these two alternatives: we talk about transubstantiation, consubstantiation, spiritual presence, memorialist views, and the like. And in the next essay, I hope to unpack in a little more detail the way I think we should approach the question of real presence. For now, though, let me simply suggest that the most helpful way to classify approaches to the Lord's Supper is by speaking of participatory and non-participatory views.

A non-participatory view separates both vertically and horizontally what happens in the celebration of communion. Vertically, such a view separates the celebration on earth from the celebration in heaven. Horizontally, such a view separates our table fellowship both from what happened on the Cross and from the marriage supper we will one day enjoy in the hereafter. In the light of what I have argued so far, it will be clear that on such a view the Eucharist cannot be sacrificial in character; for such a view separates our Eucharistic celebration vertically from the heavenly one and horizontally from what happened in the Upper Room and from the marriage feast of the Lamb. If we isolate our Eucharistic celebration in this way, both vertically and horizontally, then to say that it is sacrificial would immediately mean that we have added a second sacrifice in addition to that of Christ, which then also would be a separate or isolated sacrifice. That is why a non-participatory view invariably shies away from sacrificial language when it comes to the Eucharist. By contrast, because a participatory view holds that there is both a vertical link with heavenly worship and a horizontal link with the Cross and with the eschatological marriage supper, a participatory view can only look to this table fellowship while at the same time recognizing that it genuinely participates in the realities that it depicts or represents. If, as Torrance and Hunsinger put it, the Cross is the "depth dimension" of the Eucharist, and if the Cross is a sacrifice, then it must be true that the Eucharist participates *in the sacrifice* of the Cross. As Torrance puts it: "[B]y its very nature, therefore, the Eucharist, while being the worship of men on earth, is essentially a participation in the worship of the heavenly sanctuary which Jesus Christ their ascended High Priest renders to the Father in the oblation of his endless life ...."[34] The entire biblical logic of participation—the logic of John 15, of Colossians 1, and of Genesis 22—requires us to think of the Eucharist as a sacrificial meal, as participation in the once-for-all sacrifice of Christ.

Second, there is a specific instance of this participatory or sacramental logic at work in connection with the Passover. I have been struck for some time by the fact that the early church unanimously regarded the Eucharist as sacrificial in nature. It is there as early as the *Didache*, Clement, Justin, Irenaeus, and Hippolytus, and it runs throughout the tradition, from the very first evidence that we have, from the second century. "There is no exception whatever," comments the liturgical scholar, Gregory Dix, "in any Christian tradition in the second century and no hint of an alternative understanding anywhere."[35] The unanimity of the tradition on this score first struck me when I read the beautiful book by J.-M.-R. Tillard, called *Flesh of the Church, Flesh of Christ*.[36] Tillard shows, from passage after passage, in theologians of both East and

---

34. Torrance, "Paschal Mystery," 110.

35. Dix, *Shape of the Liturgy*, 113. As quoted in Hunsinger, *Eucharist and Ecumenism*, 128-29.

36. J.-M.-R. Tillard, *Flesh of the Church, Flesh of Christ: At the Source of the Ecclesiology of Communion*, trans. Madeleine Beaumont (Collegeville, Minn.: Liturgical, 2001).

West, that they all were convinced that in the Eucharistic celebration, we offer on the sacrificial altar our lives to God, in and through Christ. In the East, John Chrysostom explains that our sacrificial lives of mercy must be such that they are in harmony with the sacrifice that we offer up in church; after all, the sacrifice that we offer in taking care of the poor is the very one that we also bring with us to church. Speaking of the poor as if they were our altar on which we sacrifice, Chrysostom comments:

> This altar [of the poor] is made of Christ's members themselves, and the body of the Lord becomes your altar. Venerate it: you sacrifice the victim on the flesh of the Lord. This altar [of the poor] is more awesome than the one we use here [in church], not just more than the one used in ancient times [in the Old Testament]. No, do not object. This altar [in church] is awesome because of the sacrifice laid upon it; that, the one made of alms, is even more so, not just because of the alms, but because it is the very sacrifice which makes the other awesome.[37]

For Chrysostom, our sacrificial acts of mercy add beauty and weight to our Eucharistic sacrifice. And in the West, Augustine, as he looks at Paul's exhortation to

---

37. John Chrysostom, *Homilies on Second Corinthians* 20, in Schaff, *NPNF* II/12 :374. As quoted in Tillard, *Flesh of the Church*, 69; italics omitted.

"present [our] bodies as a living sacrifice" (Rom 12:1) and discusses the various gifts that Romans 12 says each of us has in the congregation, makes this comment about our gifts: "This is the sacrifice of Christians: we, being many, are one body in Christ. And this is also the sacrifice which the church continually celebrates in the sacrament of the altar, known to the faithful, in which the church teaches that it itself is offered in the offering it makes to God."[38] For Augustine, we sacrifice ourselves—the church's gifts— on the altar in the Eucharist.

The unanimity of the Tradition on this point stems, I suspect, in an important sense from the fact that from the beginning the church read the Old Testament in the light of Christ and in the light of the church. When Christians read the narrative of the institution of the Passover in Exodus 12, they could not but make the Christological and ecclesial links. This chapter provided the Israelites with detailed commands for the celebration of the Passover. It is in the light of the newness of Christ and his church that the "depth dimension" of this passage—to use Torrance's term—came to light: Now all of a sudden, the Apostles realized what these commands were for. The lamb had to be a one-year old male without blemish (Exod 12:5)? Well, says Peter, in 1 Peter 1:19, Christ is a lamb without

---

38. Augustine, De civ. dei, X.6. As quoted in Tillard, *Flesh of the Church*, 45; italics omitted.

blemish. None of the bones of the lamb were allowed to be broken (Exod 12:46)? Well, says St. John in his Gospel, that's why the soldiers didn't break Jesus' legs, but instead pierced his side to see if he was dead (John 19:36). The blood of the lamb had to be smeared on the doorframes so that the angel would not kill the firstborn Israelites, so they would be redeemed (Exod 12:7, 22)? Well, says Peter in 1 Peter 1:18, you, too, have been "redeemed." You've been redeemed with the blood of the lamb. The bread had to be unleavened bread, showing that the Israelites were in such a hurry leaving Egypt that they couldn't wait for the bread to rise (Exod 12:8, 14-20)? Well, says Paul in 1 Corinthians 5, *you*, the believers, are the new lump of dough. And I don't want there to be any leaven mixed in with you. Instead, I want you to be pure. For, he then says, "Christ, our Passover lamb, has been sacrificed. Let us therefore celebrate the festival, not with the old leaven, the leaven of malice and evil, but with the unleavened bread of sincerity and truth" (5:7-8). In other words, malice and wickedness are the leaven that belongs in Egypt. That's what you've got to get away from; you don't want that Egyptian stuff infecting the pure dough, the bread of sincerity and truth. What's happening in the life of Jesus and in the life of the church that belongs to Jesus can be seen already in Exodus chapter 12. Now, with the new reality of Christ's death and resurrection, this chapter suddenly opens up for us. Now we suddenly realize why the Lord gave Moses all these detailed commands.

As a result, Melito of Sardis, in a fascinating sermon called *On Pascha* and written around AD 160-170 to introduce the Eucharistic Easter celebration, links the Eucharistic service both with Christ's death and with the Passover. For Melito the Passover of Exodus 12 was a "mystery" (μυστήριον) or a sacrament that already participated in the depth dimension of Christ's own sacrificial death. Melito makes this clear especially at the height of his exposition, when he addresses the angel of death directly, asking: "Tell me angel, what turned you away? The slaughter of the sheep or the life of the Lord? The death of the sheep or the type of the Lord? The blood of the sheep or the spirit of the Lord?"[39] Melito is asking here the central question: what was the origin of the salvation of the Hebrews? Was it the blood of the sheep or that of Christ? His answer is unequivocal: "It is clear that you turned away seeing the mystery of the Lord in the sheep and the life of the Lord in the slaughter of the sheep and the type of the Lord in the death of the sheep. Therefore you struck not

---

39. Melito of Sardis, *On Pascha: With the Fragments of Melito and Other Material Related to the Quartodecimans*, trans. and ed. Alistair Stewart-Sykes (Crestwood, NY: St Vladimir's Seminary Press, 2001), par. 32.

Israel down, but made Egypt alone childless."[40] For Melito, the Passover celebration of the Hebrews participates mystically or sacramentally in the reality of Christ's sacrifice. The two historical events move into each other, and it is the eternal, immortal character of the Christological reality that infuses the temporal and provisional Passover of Exodus 12 with its saving power. Christ, says Melito, was the depth dimension hidden in the story of the exodus:

> This is the lamb slain,
>   this is the speechless lamb,
>   this is the one born of Mary fair ewe,
>   this is the one taken from the flock,
>   and led to slaughter.
>   Who was sacrificed in the evening,
>   and buried at night;
>   who was not broken on the tree,
>   who was not undone in the earth,
>   who rose from the dead and resurrected humankind from the grave below.[41]

The participatory kind of theology at work in Melito—based, as we have seen, on the New Testament's own appropriation of various elements of Exodus 12—

---

40. Ibid., par. 33.
41. Ibid., par. 71.

could not but lead to a sacrificial understanding of the Eucharist. "This is the lamb slain,//this is the speechless lamb"—these words could be said not just of the Passover, not just of Christ's death on the Cross, but also of the Eucharist. Passover and Eucharist both participate in the Paschal mystery of the Cross.[42] Thus, it is in the celebration of the Eucharist that heaven opens up and time gets taken up into eternity, so that the once-for-all sacrifice of Christ is yet again made present as in Christ and through the Spirit we offer up ourselves along with all our gifts in thankfulness to God. Thus, it is at the altar, around the table, that we join Christ and his apostles, that we join old Bishop Polycarp, that we join all the angels and saints in sacrificial worship in the Upper Room.

---

42. Cf. Hunsinger, *Eucharist and Ecumenism*, 128-86.

2

Eucharist and Space: Why Participation Means Real Presence

Christ and the Church: One Body

Few passages are quoted as often in the Christian tradition in connection with the Eucharist as 1 Corinthians 10:16-17. Time and again, these two verses come up in discussion as people have tried to come to grips with the meaning of what we do around this table, around this altar: "The cup of blessing that we bless, is it not a participation in the blood of Christ? The bread that we break, is it not a participation in the body of Christ? Because there is one bread, we who are many are one body, for we all partake of the one bread." There are at least two reasons for the prominence of this passage. First, Paul emphatically speaks about "participation" or "fellowship" (κοινωνία). And second, he refers to the body of Christ. Twice, in fact, he does so. The first time in verse 16: "The bread ... is it not a participation in the *body of Christ*?" And then again in verse 17: "Because there is one bread, we who are many are one *body* ...." The interesting thing is that even though we have the word "body" twice here, in very close proximity to each other, there seems to be a difference in nuance when it comes to the two occurrences of the word. When he says that the bread is a "participation in the body of Christ" (in verse 16), the Apostle seems to be talking about the historical body of Christ, which is somehow present in the Eucharistic celebration; after all, he places this "participation in the body of Christ" side by side with "participation in the blood of Christ." By mentioning "blood" alongside "body," the Apostle makes clear that in the Eucharistic service we somehow participate in Christ as the one who died for us; it is *his* body and *his* blood that Paul is talking about. But when in verse 17 he again uses the word "body," the word is used differently. Here it is the congregation of Corinth who are the "body." "Because there is one bread, *we* who are many are one body ...." "Body" in verse 16, so it seems, is a reference to Christ, while "body" in verse 17 is a reference to the church.

Now, it seems to me that we cannot separate Christ from his church. Together, as members of Christ, we make up what St. Augustine would often call the *totus Christus*, the whole Christ—made up of all the members.[43] Therefore, when we say "Christ" we inevitably say "church," and when we say "church" we say "Christ." The two belong inseparably together. And one of the reasons chapter 10:16-17 became so prominent in the history of Christian thought is that people recognized that even though the word "body" carries two distinct nuances of meaning in verses 16 and 17, St. Paul nevertheless uses the same word in both verses. He can hardly have had in mind two completely different bodies. There must be some close relationship between the "body" of Christ in verse 16 and the "body" of the church in verse 17. Theologically, there is hardly even a need to explicitly draw attention to this close link. Indeed, for much of the Christian tradition—Catholic and Protestant alike—it was obvious that one could only have fellowship with Christ by belonging to the church: *extra ecclesiam nulla salus*—"outside the church there is no salvation."[44] That is to say, if you wanted access

---

43. Cf. Jason Byassee, *Praise Seeking Understanding: Reading the Psalms with Augustine* (Grand Rapids: Eerdmans, 2007), 54-96.

44. This saying of the third-century African theologian, Cyprian, is still echoed throughout the Reformation period. See John Calvin, *Inst.* IV.1.4 ("[A]way from her bosom one cannot hope for any forgiveness of sins or any salvation"); Belgic Confession, Art. 28 ("We believe that since this holy assembly and congregation is the gathering of those who are saved and there is no salvation apart from it, no one ought to withdraw

to Christ, you had to be where Christ gave himself—in the church, that is. Theologically, Christology and ecclesiology went hand in hand.

In the first essay, I dealt with "Eucharist and Time," and I showed that the participation in Christ that we are given in the Eucharistic celebration is possible because time itself gets reconfigured around the table. Past, present, and future merge into one, since in Christ himself, ordinary, chronological time comes to participate in the eternity of God. And I made the point that this reconfiguration of time in the Eucharist means that we need to think of participation in Christ in sacrificial terms. In this essay, I will be dealing with "Eucharist and Space." So, we'll move from temporal categories—the topic of the first presentation—to spatial categories. And I will be making two basic points. The first is that just as time gets reconfigured in the Eucharist, so too space gets reconfigured. In other words, it's not just the horizontal axis—of past, present, and future—that is affected by Christ taking on flesh, but it's also the vertical axis—the heaven-and-earth relationship that gets transformed. That's why the topic for this essay is "Eucharist and Space." The second point I hope to make is that this reconfiguration of space through

---

from it, content to be by himself, regardless of his status or condition"); Westminster Confession of Faith, art. 25 ("out of which there is no ordinary possibility of salvation").

participation in Christ means that we need some sort of doctrine of real presence. If in and through the Eucharist our spatial categories are transcended, this can only be because Christ is truly or really present in our midst. All of this is, I think, implied in these two little verses of St. Paul that I have already mentioned—1 Corinthians 10:16 and 17. And that explains why theologians throughout history have been so keen to understand this passage right: a good understanding of these verses tells us a great deal about what is happening in the Eucharistic service.

1 Corinthians 8-10: Two Opposing Kinds of Participation

To get to both of these points, we need to see these two verses in the broader context of chapters 8-10. These chapters form very much a unit, as Paul is addressing here the issue of eating food that has been sacrificed to idols. Chapter 8:1—"Now concerning food offered to idols…." Presumably, this is something that the Corinthians have asked Paul about; it's an issue in the congregation.[45] Of course, it is not the first time the issue comes up. About five or six years earlier, the Jerusalem Council (AD 49/50)

---

45. Compare St. Paul's Περὶ δὲ τῶν εἰδωλοθύτον (8:1) with Περὶ δὲ ὧν ἐγράψατε (7:1), Περὶ δὲ τῶν πνευματικῶν (12:1), and Περὶ δὲ τῆς λογείας τῆς εἰς τοὺς ἁγίους (16:1).

had decided in response to a request for advice from Antioch that they should "abstain from the things polluted by idols" (Acts 15:20). The question of how this general guideline should be implemented in the church of Corinth was a matter of considerable difficulty. Throughout much of the discussion in these three chapters, St. Paul appears to side with those who think that eating food offered to idols is not really a problem. Those in Corinth who claim that it's fine to eat such sacrificial food—perhaps even eat it in an idol's temple (8:9)—do so on the basis of the correct "knowledge" that "an idol has no real existence" (8:4). St. Paul in no way denies this: "[W]e know that 'an idol has no real existence,' and that 'there is no God but one.'" He nonetheless injects a word of caution, since not everyone has this correct knowledge: "However, not all possess this knowledge. But some, through former association with idols, eat food as really offered to an idol, and their conscience, being weak, is defiled" (8:7). Clearly, though he is warning the so-called "knowledgeable" Corinthians against eating, he is in no way disagreeing with their theological knowledge, based on the Shema of Deuteronomy 6:4, that "there is no God but one." Put differently, Paul's argument against eating sacrificial food is by way of concession to the lack of knowledge that would make it wrong for the weak brother to eat sacrificial food against his conscience (8:7).

What is more, when St. Paul then turns to a personal illustration by way of interlude, in chapter 9, he makes clear that he himself has various sorts of "rights" (ἐξουσίαι) that he nonetheless doesn't make use of. The Apostle has a "right" to food and drink, has a "right" to travel with a believing wife, and has a "right" not to have to work for a living (9:4-6). He elaborates on this latter issue with an interesting appeal to Old Testament Law (Deut 25:4; 1 Cor 9:9) and concludes in verse 12: "Nevertheless, we have not made use of this right." And again in verse 15: "But I have made no use of any of these rights." And then we get this famous passage in which Paul says that despite his freedom, he is making himself a servant to all (9:19), becoming "as a Jew" to the Jews, becoming "as one under the law" to those under the law, and becoming "as one outside the law" to those outside the law (9:20-21). He comments in verse 22: "To the weak I became weak, that I might win the weak. I have become all things to all people, that by all means I might save some. I do it all for the sake of the gospel, that I may share with them in its blessings." This is, of course, the real issue: Paul becomes weak for the sake of the weak. Clearly, the principle of accommodation, which the Apostle articulates throughout this chapter— his willingness not to make use of what *are* his rights, and his willingness so to become weak for the weak—is based on the assumption that the weak in Corinth are in the wrong; while those who boast of their knowledge are in the right—at least, in terms of their understanding that idols don't really exist. One might well be tempted to draw the conclusion at this point—at the end of chapter 9—that there is nothing inherently wrong with eating sacrificial food at an idols' temple, and that the only reason Paul urges the Corinthians against it is the fact that love for the weak brother should make them think twice. Love, after all, is more important than knowledge. 8:1—"This 'knowledge' puffs up, but love builds up. If anyone imagines that he knows something, he does not yet know as he ought to know. But if anyone loves God, he is known by God" (8:1-3). Just because you "know" something correctly, that doesn't mean you have to act on that knowledge; love may prevent you from acting on it. That is the gist of chapters 8 and 9, it seems.

Chapter 10, however, the last chapter of this triptych, throws us a curve ball. Yes, it's true, in his conclusion the Apostle again gives some significant nods to the "knowledgeable" party in Corinth. They don't need to go to great lengths trying to ferret out what kind of meat they're dealing with. If they're not in an idol's temple, but simply in the market place or in someone's house—this is 10:25-27—they don't need to go out of their way to figure out where this meat comes from, from an idol's temple or from a regular slaughter house. After all, in those cases, there is little worry that they might cause problems for a weak brother's conscience. In such a context, there can hardly be a problem with making use of one's right to eat meat. Whether or not this is meat that was once used for cultic purposes is something that clearly doesn't concern Paul. As the Psalmist says in Psalm 24: "The earth is the Lord's, and the fullness thereof" (10:26).[46]

But the curve ball that I mentioned lies in the main section of this last chapter, in 10:1-22. Here St. Paul makes quite clear that the issue is not as straightforward as the so-called "knowledgeable" party in Corinth may think; and that, in fact, the argument he has been making is not just a matter of prudence out of consideration for the weak brother.[47] Notice that the Apostle gives us two vignettes. In the first, he gives the example from Israel's wilderness journey, and he reminds the Corinthians, first, of the fact that most of the Israelites coming from Egypt never made

---

46. Note, however, that even in this context, there is a word of caution: if there is any danger of harming another person's conscience (which may happen when one is informed in the marketplace or in someone else's house that the meat they're serving is sacrificial food), then, again, Paul counsels against eating (10:28). And the final comment again serves to ensure that one not give offense (10:32) or seek one's own advantage, but instead seek the advantage "of many, that they may be saved" (10:33).

47. Here I am broadly following Gordon D. Fee, *The First Epistle to the Corinthians* (Grand Rapids: Eerdmans, 1987), 358-59, 441.

it into the Promised Land because of their rebellion after hearing the report of the twelve spies, in Numbers 14 (1 Cor 10:5); and then of several additional examples where God had punished the people for their idolatry, their testing, and their grumbling (10:7-10).

One thing stands out in this first vignette: the examples centre on cultic worship. Paul is not just pulling on any old example from the Old Testament wilderness journey. No, he keeps in mind the issue at hand: eating food sacrificed to idols in an idol's temple. It is despite their baptismal and Eucharistic identity—10:2-3 ("all were baptized into Moses in the cloud and in the sea, and all ate the same spiritual food, and all drank the same spiritual drink")—that God was not pleased with the Israelites and overthrew them. And it is the idolatry of the Israelites at Baal Peor (10:7; cf. Num 25:2-3) that led to 23,000 Israelites being killed on a single day (10:8).[48]

---

48. In 1 Cor 10:9, Paul indicates that according to Num 21—the narrative about the bronze snake—the Israelites "put Christ to the test." According to Num 21, the Israelites spoke against the LORD and against Moses (21:5, 7). In 1 Cor 10:10, the Apostle warns the Corinthians not to "grumble, as some of them did and were destroyed by the Destroyer," referring to the narrative of Korah, Dathan, and Abiram along with their followers, whose worship (in the form of burning incense) was not accepted by God. Particularly in this last example, the cultic context is clear, though St. Paul does not mention it explicitly.

The Israelites' disobedience had to do with idolatry—something that is obviously a possibility, regardless of the Corinthian "knowledgeable" claim that idols do not exist. St. Paul appears to be intimating that maybe there is more to this issue of eating sacrificial food in the temple than he has let on so far—that, in fact, it could be an issue of momentous significance.

That this is indeed the case, is something St. Paul makes explicit in the second vignette, that of the verses 14-22, when he draws his conclusion of the historical examples with the dramatic words: "Therefore, my beloved, flee from idolatry" (10:14). When he began his discussion, back in 8:4, he seemed to be agreeing with those in Corinth who were "in the know": "[W]e know that 'an idol has no real existence' ..." (8:4). Now, however, he warns them to "flee from idolatry." Even though there is no εἴδωλον, no idol, there is εἰδωλολατρία, idolatry. How can this be? How do we rhyme 8:4 with 10:14? How do we rhyme the notion that idols don't exist with the strong exhortation to flee from idolatry? We find the answer in the verses 19 and 20. In those few lines St. Paul completely cuts the ground from under what now turns out to have been a ridiculous argument—namely, that the Corinthians can participate in the sacrificial cult simply because idols don't exist. The argument is absurd because, Paul says in these verses, even though idols don't exist, demons do![49] And "what pagans sacrifice they offer to demons and not to God" (10:20). The juvenile claim that idols don't exist completely ignores that it is possible to be participants with demons and that, just as with ancient Israel, the question is: are you going to have participation in the body and blood of Christ, or are you going to have participation in demons (10:16, 20)?

This is a dramatic turn in the argument. Whereas for the most part, St. Paul had appeared to side with those Corinthians whose so-called "knowledge" allowed them to participate in the sacrificial cult of the idols' temples, with these two vignettes he clarifies that the matter is actually far more serious than he has thus far been prepared to let on. One either partakes in the Eucharistic feast, or one participates in cultic idolatry. One either has communion with Christ, or one has communion with demons. The Corinthians cannot have it both ways.

---

49. Cf. David Prior, *The Message of 1 Corinthians: Life in the Local Church* (Leicester, UK: Inter-Varsity, 1985), 174: "Paul is not reversing his original denial that 'food offered to idols is anything' or that 'an idol is anything'. He still affirms the non-entity, the un-reality of idols as such; but he equally affirms that behind all idolatry is demonic activity: *What pagans sacrifice they offer to demons and not to God* (20)."

Participatory vs. Non-participatory Views

We are now closing in on the two verses that we started out with, the verses 16 and 17. And I suspect that in the light of what we have seen so far, these two verses will, in some way, speak for themselves. The Apostle is contrasting two kinds of participation or communion: on the one hand, participation in the blood of Christ and the body of Christ (verse 16), and on the other hand, participation with demons (verse 20). We need to take this notion of "participation" or "communion," which Paul mentions here, quite seriously.[50] This notion allows Paul to switch

---

50. Some commentators draw attention to the fact that Paul is using the term κοινωνία, which is often translated as "fellowship" or "communion," rather than the terms μετουσία or μετοχή, which were technical philosophical terms often used to speak of "participation"—and these commentators imply that Paul eschews the more radical Platonic notion of μετοχή, which implies ontological change. Perhaps there is a difference between the two terms. But if so, we should take note of what *kind* of difference it might be. St. John Chrysostom, as he comments on verse 16, makes the following interesting observation: "'The bread which we break, is it not a communion of the Body of Christ?' Wherefore said he not, the participation?" Chrysostom is asking here: why is Paul speaking of κοινωνία rather than μετοχή? And his answer is as follows: "Because he [Paul] intended to express something more and to point out

from the "body" meaning Christ in verse 16 to the "body"

---

how close was the union: in that we communicate not only by participating and partaking, but also by being united. For as that body is united to Christ, so also are we united to him by this bread" (John Chrysostom, *Homilies on First Corinthians*, in Philip Schaff, ed., *Nicene and Post-Nicene Fathers*, I/12 [1889, repr.; Peabody, Mass., 1994], 139-40; cf. J.-M.-R. Tillard, *Flesh of the Church, Flesh of Christ: At the Source of the Ecclesiology of Communion*, trans. Madeleine Beumont [Collegeville, Minn.: Liturgical, 2001], 67). Archibald Robertson and Alfred Plummer (appealing to John Chrysostom) maintain, "The difference between 'participation' and 'fellowship' or 'communion' is the difference between having a share and having the whole. In Holy Communion each recipient has a share of the bread and of the wine, but he has the whole of Christ ..." (*A Critical and Exegetical Commentary on the First Epistle of St Paul to the Corinthians*, 2nd ed. (Edinburgh: T & T Clark, 1914), 212. So, for Chrysostom at least, the term κοινωνία bespeaks a close, real union, which is effected by means of one's eating of the bread and drinking of the cup—a union closer and more real than would have been intimated by means of terms such as μετουσία or μετοχή. So, the difference is not that the philosophical term μετοχή would actually unite the participant and the participated into one; whereas the biblical notion of κοινωνία would leave the two subjects of the fellowship independent, separate from each other. If anything, the difference is the opposite. I am not sure how far we need to push this distinction between the two Greek terms. What is clear, however, is that the κοινωνία that St. Paul speaks about leads one into an actual union, either with meaning the church in verse 17. The Eucharist establishes a real communion or participation with Christ and so makes us literally participate in him. In chapter 12, the Apostle will reflect at length on what it means that now, by participating in the body, we have become the body. He speaks in that chapter about spiritual gifts and argues that the many parts of the body—the foot, the hand, the ear, the eye, the head, and the feet—all have their part to play in the body. The basic theological reason, according to St. Paul in 12:12 is this: "For just as the body is one and has many members, and all the members of the body, though many, are one body, so it is with Christ. For in one Spirit we were all baptized into one body— Jews or Greeks, slaves or free—and all were made to drink of one Spirit." Notice how he puts it in verse 12. He doesn't say: "Just as the body is one and has many members, so it is with the *church*." No, he says, "… so it is with *Christ*." Christ himself is made up of many members. It appears that for Paul, in an important sense at least, the *church* is Christ. As I indicated in the previous essay, it is together that we make up St. Augustine's so-called *totus Christus*. When in chapter 12 St. Paul uses the metaphor of a body made up of many members, he is not just using a rather indifferent

---

Christ's body and blood or with demons. We should also note that St. Paul repeatedly uses the verb μετέχειν in the immediate context (9:10, 12; 10:21, 30).

metaphor, one that could fit any other organization just as well as the church—so that we could talk of the church as one social organization among many; so that just as there is an ecclesial body, so too there are economic bodies, juridical bodies, political bodies, etc. That broader use of the term "body" isn't necessarily wrong-headed,[51] but it is important to remember that the church is a "body" in ways that no other organization is. The church is a body primarily because the church is connected to the sacramental, Eucharistic body of Christ. It is Christ's body in the Eucharist—mentioned in 10:16—that leads to the reality of Christ's body in the church—mentioned in 10:17.

---

51. We do need to keep in mind, however, that there is a historical link between the loss of a link between Eucharist and church, on the one hand, and the rise of this secular use of "body" language since around the twelfth century. See Ernst Hartwig Kantorowicz, *The King's Two Bodies: A Study in Mediaeval Political Theology* (Princeton: Princeton University Press, 1957), 197; Bryan C. Hollon, *Everything Is Sacred: Spiritual Exegesis in the Political Theology of Henri de Lubac*, Theopolitical Visions, 3 (Eugene, Ore.: Cascade, 2009), 65. Cf. Henri de Lubac, *Corpus Mysticum: The Eucharist and the Church in the Middle Ages: Historical Survey*, trans. Gemma Simmonds with Richard Price and Christopher Stephens, ed. Laurence Paul Hemming and Susan Frank Parsons (London: SCM, 2006), 85.

Eucharistic Participation

In the first essay, I mentioned that there are broadly two approaches to understanding the Eucharist: a participatory and a non-participatory one. I should probably at this point elaborate on what I mean by that. Briefly put, a non-participatory view separates heaven and earth, while a participatory view sees earth as participating in heavenly realities. On a non-participatory understanding—and those are views that become increasingly prominent in the early modern period—earth is below and heaven above, and so the two are not really connected. While communication may still be possible between heaven and earth, by means of human prayer to God or by means of God's supernatural involvement in earthly affairs, those are regarded more or less as ad hoc, external interventions. The implication, for the Eucharist, is that it would seem odd to think of Christ as being really present in the elements or to say that the elements are somehow transformed into the body of Christ. The sign or the *signum* (the bread) is here below; and the reality or the *res* (the body of Christ), to which the sign points, is above. Sign and reality, bread and body are separated much like heaven and earth are separated. To take Jesus' saying, "This is my body" (Matt 26:26; 1 Cor 11:24), in anything more than a metaphorical sense would seem, on such a view, to lapse into crass literalism. And because the bread is not the body, this view takes a memorialist understanding of the Lord's Supper: in the Supper, we remember (in line with 1 Corinthians

11:24-25) what Christ did in giving his life for us. Such a view has become more and more common, not only among free-church traditions but also among Calvinists, who seem to be increasingly backing away from Calvin's much more robust, and in some way participatory view, toward a much more non-participatory, memorialist view.[52] My reading of 1 Corinthians 10:16-17 leads to a more participatory view of what happens in the Eucharist. On this view, our participation in the body and blood of

---

52. Calvin and the later Reformed confessions could use remarkably strong language that nearly seemed to imply a "real presence" and a participation or mutual indwelling of sign and reality. Chapter XXI of the Scots Confession, alluding specifically to the spatial distance between heaven and earth, states: "Notwithstanding the distance between his glorified body in heaven and mortal men on earth, yet we must assuredly believe that the bread which we break is the communion of Christ's body and the cup which we bless the communion of his blood. Thus we confess and believe without doubt that the faithful, in the right use of the Lord's Table, do so eat the body and drink the blood of the Lord Jesus that he remains in them and they in him; they are so made flesh of his flesh and bone of his bone that as the eternal Godhood has given to the flesh of Christ Jesus, which by nature was corruptible and mortal, life and immortality, so the eating and drinking of the flesh and blood of Christ Jesus does the like for us." (For additional Reformed confessional examples, see George Hunsinger, *The Eucharist and Ecumenism* (Cambridge: Cambridge University Press, 2008), 49.

Christ in the Eucharist (mentioned in verse 16), makes us into the very body of Christ (mentioned in verse 17). Or, we could also say, along with one of my favourite theologians, Henri de Lubac: the Eucharist makes the church.[53]

George Hunsinger, the well-known Reformed theologian from Princeton, in his book, *The Eucharist and Ecumenism*, relates how he came to his participatory view of the Eucharist:

> Looking back, it seems that the turning point came in 1995 during a Lenten Bible study in my local congregation. Feeling that my New Testament Greek, never very good, was getting ever more rusty by the day, I took an interlinear volume with me to one of the sessions. To my surprise the word *koinonia* [fellowship, participation] showed up in 1 Cor. 10:16. Could it be, I wondered, that the relationship between the bread and Christ's body might be one of mutual indwelling? Over time my hunch was reinforced by Luther, confirmed by Vermigli, and validated by Käsemann.[54]

---

53. See especially de Lubac, *Corpus Mysticum*. Cf. Hans Boersma, *Nouvelle Théologie and Sacramental Ontology: A Return to Mystery* (Oxford: Oxford University Press, 2009), 247-55.

54. Hunsinger, *Eucharist and Ecumenism*, viii-ix.

Hunsinger's discovery of this Pauline passage, which has been crucial in the history of biblical interpretation, allowed him to accept a more robust participatory or sacramental view of the Eucharist. Hunsinger might well have learned this same lesson from St. Augustine. In Sermon 227, the African Bishop says the following about consuming Christ's body and blood: "If you receive them well, you are yourselves what you receive. You see, the apostle says, *We, being many, are one loaf, one body* (1 Cor 10:17)."[55] The comment sounds innocuous enough, but it contains two fascinating elements. First, when we talk about transubstantiation—the Catholic doctrine that the substance of the elements changes in the Eucharist—we naturally think of the teaching that the bread becomes the body of Christ. St. Augustine says something rather different. He maintains, *You* become the body of Christ; *you* become what you eat. We could perhaps say, somewhat anachronistically: for Augustine, transubstantiation means that the Spirit changes *our* substance into the body of Christ.

---

55. Augustine, "Sermon 227," in *Sermons, (184-229Z) on the Liturgical Seasons*, vol. III/6 of *The Works of Saint Augustine*, trans. Edmund Hill, ed. John E. Rotelle (New Rochelle, NY: New City, 1993), 254. The following two paragraphs follow Hans Boersma, *Heavenly Participation: The Weaving of a Sacramental Tapestry* (Grand Rapids: Eerdmans, 2011), 113-14.

This would seem like a peculiar understanding of the Eucharist. What does St. Augustine mean when he says, "You are what you have received?" To find an answer to this question, we need to turn to the second fascinating element in Augustine's comment. In the second part of his statement, the Bishop of Hippo quotes the Apostle Paul: "You see, the apostle says, *We, being many, are one loaf, one body.*" This is a quotation from 1 Corinthians 10:17. Augustine recognizes that St. Paul places the Eucharistic body and the ecclesial body right beside each other in the verses 16 and 17. And so, St. Augustine paraphrases it by saying: we become what we have received. Or, we could again say: the Eucharist makes the church. The communion or the unity of the church is the very reason why we celebrate the Eucharist. The Eucharist unites us into one.

Participation as Trans-elementation

So far, I have followed 1 Corinthians 10:16-17, and I have linked the Eucharistic body with the ecclesial body. What I have not yet done is to explore how the elements of communion (the Eucharistic body) participate in the ascended body of our Lord. I have not yet explained how earthly realities can participate in heavenly ones and, in particular, how the *signum* or sign here below (the elements) can participate in the *res* or reality above (the body of Christ). Perhaps the best thing to do is to begin with St. Paul's theology of heaven in Ephesians and Colossians.[56] For Paul, it is not as though believers here on earth somehow identify with a far-away place called "heaven." Rather, they have a real or participatory connection with heaven. The central paschal event—Christ's death, resurrection, and ascension—is something in which Christians participate: God "made us alive with Christ," insists Paul (Eph 2:5). He "raised us up with Christ" (Eph 2:6; cf. Col 3:1). The result of this sharing in Christ is that believers participate in heavenly realities. We are seated with Christ "in the heavenly realms in Christ Jesus" (Eph 2:6; cf. 1:3). What this means is that we should take our place in heaven—participating in Christ—much more seriously than often we do. In an important sense, we are in heaven in a much more real sense than we are on earth. And I don't mean that in just a metaphorical sense, so that we could talk *as if* we were in heaven. No, when St. Paul says that we have been made alive with Christ, have been raised up with Christ, and are seated with Christ in heaven, he is using the language of participation. He means that, already, through faith and the gift of the Holy Spirit, our place really is in heaven; we have a real presence in heaven.[57] Any imagined

---

56. The following brief section is taken from Boersma, *Heavenly Participation*, 4-5.

57. That faith and the gift of the Holy Spirit are the means to enter into heaven implies that we need *both* the Reformation

separation between heaven and earth, or between nature and the supernatural, gets undone in Jesus Christ. And since it is in Christ that this happens, it is through the preaching and the sacrament that we are taken up into the heavenly places.

Not only, however, is there an upward movement—so that the pastor or the priest can say with St. Paul in the Eucharistic celebration: "Lift up your hearts," and we respond by saying, "We lift them up to the Lord"—but there is also a downward movement, in the sense that we follow our Lord in saying, "This is the body of Christ." In other words, just as in the Eucharist time gets taken up into eternity—so, too, space gets reconfigured: the earthly reality of bread, we could say, gets taken up into the heavenly reality of Christ. In what follows, I want to briefly turn to the fourth-century theologian, Gregory of Nyssa. He describes what happens in the Eucharist by means of four steps.[58] First, Gregory explains that food and drink,

---

emphasis on the need for a partaking of the Eucharist in faith *and* the emphasis of the Great Tradition on our being changed into the Body of Christ as a result of our partaking. Our sanctification is both the prerequisite and the result of a fruitful participation in the Eucharist. Hence my emphasis on *epiklēsis* in the earlier presentation on "Eucharist and Time."

58. Most of the discussion of these four steps is taken from Hans Boersma, *Embodiment and Virtue in Gregory of Nyssa:*

by entering into our bodies (and he is talking about regular eating and drinking here), change into our bodies: "For by passing into me those elements become body and blood, seeing that the nourishment by transformative (ἀλλοιωτικῆς) power is changed (μεθισταμένης) in each case into the form (εἶδος) of the body."[59] Notice Gregory's language of "transformation" and "change," already in connection with regular eating. He is making the point that in the process of nourishment, the various material "elements" of food change into the form of the body. That word "elements"—στοιχεῖα is the Greek word Gregory uses—is a term I want to get back to in a little while. So,

---

An Anagogical Approach (Oxford: Oxford University Press, 2013), ch. 6. Cf. the discussions in S. de Boer, *De anthropologie van Gregorius van Nyssa* (Assen: Van Gorcum, 1968), 289-96; Reinhard Jakob Kees, *Die Lehre von der Oikonomia Gottes in der Oratio catechetica Gregors von Nyssa*, Supplements to Vigiliae Christianae, 30 (Leiden: Brill, 1995), 182-91; Lucas Francisco Mateo-Seco, 'Eucharist', in *The Brill Dictionary of Gregory of Nyssa*, ed. Lucas Francisco Mateo-Seco and Giulio Maspero, trans. Seth Cherney (Leiden: Brill, 2009).

59. *Oratio catechetica magna* (*Or cat*), ed. Ekkehardus Mühlenberg (*Gregorii Nysseni Opera* III/4), 95.20-23; ET: *The Catechetical Oration of St. Gregory of Nyssa* (hereafter Srawley), ed. and trans. J. H. Srawley, Early Church Classics (London: Society for Promoting Christian Knowledge, 1917), 109-10; translation slightly adjusted.

the first step is that the elements of food change into the form of our body.

Second, Gregory then applies this general principle to Christ. In his case, too, his body was in some sense identical with the food that he used to eat.[60] So, we could say that in a literal sense, when Christ ate, bread would change into the body of Christ. In the case of Christ, however, says Gregory, there is a second transformation due to the fact that in the Incarnation the Word of God has assumed the human body. The Incarnation—the Word of God taking on human flesh—means, says Gregory, that "the Body, through the indwelling of God, was translated (μετεποιήθη) to the dignity of the Godhead."[61] The indwelling of the Word "sanctified" (ἡγιάσθη), he also says, Christ's body.[62] Put differently, Christ's body became immortal, was divinized, because it was assumed by the eternal Word. The Word's assumption of the body changes the body and makes it holy, renders it immortal, divinizes it. So, we could say that in the case of Christ, there is a twofold change or transformation: first from food and drink to body—something we all experience when we eat and drink—and then from body to divinized body, because of

---

60. *Or cat* 96.13-18 (Srawley 110).
61. *Or cat* 96.20-22 (Srawley 110).
62. *Or cat* 97.1 (Srawley 111).

the union between the eternal Word and the human body in the Incarnation.

This of course raises the question of how the second transformation in Christ (the change of his body to being divinized) can take place also in ordinary human beings like us. Here Gregory's question is: how do we become holy? How do we come to participate in the life of God? How do we become immortal? In other words, this is the question of our salvation: how do we come to share in Christ? How do we come to sit with him in the heavenly places at the right hand of God? In the third step of his argument, St. Gregory addresses these questions through a discussion of what happens in the Eucharist. Here, explains Gregory, we again have bread changing into the body of Christ. But, of course, in the Eucharist, we—not Christ—are the ones who do the eating. And so, Gregory says that in the Eucharist the change happens not by eating the bread. No, says Gregory, the bread doesn't have to wait to be eaten before it is changed or sanctified so as to become the body of Christ. In the Eucharist, the bread becomes the body of Christ through the combination of God's promise, "This is my body" and the invocation (the *epiklēsis*) of the Holy Spirit. The bread, says Gregory, "is transmuted (μεταποιούμενος) immediately into the Body through the Word, even as the Word has said, 'This is my Body' [Matt 26:26 par.]."[63]

This finally leads Gregory to his fourth and final step. By eating the sanctified, transformed elements, what we do, in fact, is: we eat the deified body of Christ. God, says Gregory, "plants Himself, in accordance with His plan of grace, in all believers by means of that Flesh, which derives its subsistence from both wine and bread, mingling (κατακιρνάμενος) Himself with the bodies of believers, in order that, by union with that which is immortal, man might also participate (μέτοχος) in incorruption."[64] Thus, it is through the "transforming" (μεταστοιχειώσας) of bread and wine[65] that God also changes us. In other words, the bread has been transformed into the sanctified or deified body of Christ, and because we eat the immortal body of Christ, we, too, are changed and come to participate in the life of God.[66] Christ's Eucharistic body thus

---

63. *Or cat* 97.5-12 (Srawley 111).
64. *Or cat* 98.1-6 (Srawley 112).
65. *Or cat* 98.7 (Srawley 112).
66. As Norman Russell puts it: "The humanity that was deified was the flesh of Christ. But that flesh is the same flesh that believers receive in communion. The Eucharist thus enables them to participate in the deifying effect of the Incarnation" (Norman Russell, *The Doctrine of Deification in the Greek Patristic Tradition* [Oxford: Oxford University Press, 2004], 228). For insightful discussion of deification in Gregory, see Lewis

"transforms and changes" (μεταποεῖ καὶ μετατίθησιν) our bodies to become like his.[67]

There is a lot of "transformation" and "change" language here. In fact, there are four stages of "change." Gregory uses different Greek words, all describing the same kind of process. He use verbs such as μεθίστημι (which literally put is something like "translate" or "reposition" or "move over"), μεταποιέω (which, again literally, says something like "transmute," or "remake" or "remodel"), μετατίθημι (something like "to replace," or "to transpose"). Perhaps most important—if we think of the later history of Christian thought—Gregory speaks of μεταστοιχείωσις (a changing of the elements; trans-elementation, we could say). The general drift of what Gregory is doing is probably becoming clear.

Now, much of this may sound like Gregory is simply talking about basic, physical changes. And, in some sense he is. In the first step, when the elements (the στοιχεῖα) of food change into our bodies, that's an ordinary physical change. But, in the second step, when the Word becomes incarnate and translates or transforms Christ's body, then Gregory suddenly uses sanctification language (ἁγιάζω).

Ayres, "Deification and the Dynamics of Nicene Theology: The Contribution of Gregory of Nyssa," *St Vladimir's Theological Quarterly* 49 (2005), 375-94.

67. *Or cat* 94.1 (Srawley 107-08); my translation.

This change is one that changes Christ's body to make it holy so that it is suitable for the indwelling of the eternal Word. And in the fourth and final step, when we eat this sanctified body of Christ, we as a result, too, are sanctified in and with Christ. Or, as Gregory also puts it, we come to participate— μέτοχος is the word—in the very immortality of Christ. Notice the language that Gregory uses: "sanctification," "participation." When the eternal Word assumes a human body in the Incarnation, the human body participates in the Word, gets sanctified in the Word. And as a result, when with our bodies we eat Christ's body, we come to participate in Christ, and so we too get sanctified.

Conclusion: Eucharist as Mystery

Of course, this change of ours—this sanctification or participation in the immortality of Christ—this process depends on the bread really changing into the body of Christ. We can only get sanctified and participate in the life of God if the bread has really become the body of Christ. And so the question is: what kind of a change does Gregory have in mind when he says that the bread is transmuted or transelemented into the body of Christ? The interesting thing is: Gregory doesn't say. He doesn't explain the change that takes place in connection with the Eucharist. All he says is that the change takes place as a result of Christ's word of promise ("This is my body") and as a result of the prayer of invocation that we offer up to the Holy Spirit. This strikes me as hugely significant. Sometimes we use the terms to describe what happens in the Eucharist—transubstantiation, consubstantiation, real presence, spiritual presence, and so on—in order to explain exactly what is happening. But just a moment's thought should make us realize that you and I cannot possibly describe this change. If it's true that in the Eucharist we enter heaven and heaven comes to earth, if it's true that in the liturgy we witness the opening up of heaven itself, then to say that we could capture that heavenly *res* or reality would be the ultimate display of presumption. In relation to these heavenly realities you and I are blinder than a bat in the noonday sun. Whatever the change is, it's not a change from one this-worldly substance (namely, bread), into another this-worldly substance. Earthly bread becomes heavenly manna. There is just no way you and I can explain what that means. "This is my body" is a saying whose heavenly dimension invests it with infinite depth. Words surely must fail to describe the reality beyond the sign.

This is not to say that we must completely fall silent. George Hunsinger, the Reformed theologian whose book I have already mentioned a few times, picks up on the notion of transelementation, which he shows is present not only in Gregory of Nyssa and a number of other Eastern theologians, but, interestingly, also in several Reformation theologians, such as Peter Martyr Vermigli, Martin Bucer, and Thomas Cranmer.[68] Each of these theologians used the image of an iron rod that gets thrown into the fire. Hunsinger puts it this way:

> The image which illustrated transelementation was that of an iron rod thrust into the fire. Just as the iron was transformed by its participation in the fire, so was the consecrated element transformed by its sacramental union with Christ's flesh. In and with this transforming union, the distinction between the two was maintained. Just as the iron did not cease to be iron, or the fire fire, so did the bread not cease to be bread, or Christ's flesh his flesh. In the mystery of their sacramental union they formed unique distinction-in-unity and unity-in-distinction.[69]

Note what the imagery of transformed iron does. It alludes to the "participation" language that 1 Corinthians 10:16 and Gregory of Nyssa both use: "The bread that we break, is it not a participation in the body of Christ?" The bread genuinely participates in the body of Christ. Just as

---

68. Hunsinger, *Eucharist and Ecumenism*, 40-46. Hunsinger explains that these theologians relied for the notion of "transelementation" on the eleventh-century Archbishop of Bulgaria, Theophylact.

69. Ibid., 41.

the iron participates in the fire and as a result gets changed by the fire, so the bread participates in the body of Christ and as a result gets changed by the body of Christ. That sounds very much like real presence: the fire is really present in the iron. But it's not the kind of real presence that allows us to explain what exactly is happening in this so-called "transelementation."[70] Yes, the elements change so as to be conformed to the body of Christ. But even the imagery of the iron in the fire falls short at the crucial point. Both iron and fire are earthly realities. But although the bread is an earthly reality, the body of Christ is not. Christ's body has been raised from the dead and has ascended into heaven. His body is a heavenly body (cf. 1 Cor 15:48-49). The metaphor of the iron in the fire is helpful because it allows us to illustrate the participation of which St. Paul speaks in 1 Corinthians 10. But it is no more than a metaphor. At the crucial point, the point where we would perhaps hope to "explain" transelementation, the metaphor falls short.

---

70. The use of the language of "presence" is relatively recent. St. Thomas avoids this language, as it may bind the body of Christ too closely to a this-worldly location. See Jean-Yves Lacoste, "Presence and Parousia," trans. A. J. Wickens, in *The Blackwell Companion to Postmodern Theology*, ed. Graham Ward (Malden, Mass.: Blackwell, 2005), 394-98, at 395.

EUCHARISTIC PARTICIPATION

While I believe we should positively affirm participation and real presence in connection with the Eucharist—as is implied in 1 Corinthians 10, in the overall biblical teaching of participation, and in the history of Christian teaching on this topic—I have also tried to highlight the fact that the language of participation has its limits. That is to say, when space itself gets reconfigured by earthly bread participating in heavenly manna, we cannot expect rationally to comprehend fully what goes on in the Eucharist.[71] Participation language alludes to the fact that the Eucharist is a mystery that we enter into rather than a puzzle that we try to solve. In some sense, all Christian doctrine is like that. It doesn't try so much rationally to explain in this-worldly terms as to use reason to allow us to enter into an other-worldly reality. In that sense, doctrine merely sets boundaries against explanations that try to rationally comprehend the truth in this-worldly, earthly terms. That kind of rationalism, it seems to me, would be the result if we tried to understand the Eucharist in such a way that we had spatially captured Christ in the element. Although I think it is fair to say that Thomas Aquinas

---

71. Herbert McCabe puts it well: "We are dealing here with something that transcends our concepts and can only be spoken of by stretching language to breaking point. We are dealing here with mystery" ("Eucharistic Change," in *God Still Matters*, ed. Brian Davies [London: Continuum], 115-22, at 117).

cautiously guards against this danger, we do need to be watchful with transubstantiation. We should not think that the bread gets changed into another, this-worldly substance—a danger that I worry is difficult to avoid especially in the Catholic devotional practice of adoration of the host. There is a danger of undue rationalism if and when we reduce the mystery of Eucharistic change to a this-worldly event. If we were to collapse the heavenly reality into the earthly sign so that the sign gets obliterated, as it were—so that it is no longer clear that we can still speak of the bread as being bread—it becomes difficult to use the language of participation. Participation is something different from obliteration.

At the same time, we equally need to guard against a purely mental understanding that fully explains what happens in the Lord's Supper by insisting that our link with the heavenly body of Christ is one of the mind only. The danger of much evangelical, and even certain Reformed, approaches to the Eucharist is that we reduce the relationship between bread and body to a strictly external one—where the bread is here below and the body up above. Ironically, such an approach, too, runs the danger of rationalism, since on this understanding, too, we reduce the mystery of the Eucharist to a this-worldly event, one that centres on our faith commitment and on the working of the Spirit in our hearts—all of this at the cost of genuine participation in the body of Christ. Here we certainly can speak of the bread as being bread; but we cannot with integrity speak of the bread also as the body of Christ. The iron-in-the-fire metaphor becomes difficult. Participation language no longer fits. We need to remember that participation in Christ is something quite different from mental recollection of Christ.

I started off with a discussion of the two bodies mentioned in 1 Corinthians 10:16-17, the first one being the Eucharistic body, the second one the ecclesial body. In the history of the church—especially in the Middle Ages—theologians would often speak not just of two, but of three bodies: the historical body of Christ, born of the virgin; the Eucharistic body of Christ, really present in the elements of bread and wine; and the ecclesial body, the church. Although these theologians spoke of three bodies, it will be clear by now that what they really meant is not that there are three bodies, but that there are three aspects of one and the same body—the body of Christ—just as for St. Augustine there is one totus Christus, the head and the members. In that sense, it might be better to speak of one threefold body.

We may talk a great deal about the variety of ways in which different traditions understand "presence" in connection with the Lord's Supper. And yes, this is an important discussion—though, as I said, I think the language of participation implies that we need a certain intellectual humility as we engage in these discussions. But what is really key is to remember that the three "bodies" are not really three separate bodies at all. The purpose of the Eucharist is not the change of the elements—or whatever we may think happens in connection with the elements. Transelementation, while it seems to me perhaps the best way of talking about what happens in the Eucharist, is not the purpose of the Eucharist. The purpose is not, ultimately, the change of the bread. The purpose, as St. Gregory of Nyssa well knew, is that that we be changed into the body of Christ. The ultimate reality, the ultimate purpose is our change, not that of the elements. Verse 16 of 1 Corinthians 10 gives way to verse 17. When the Spirit, through Word and sacrament, changes us to become like Christ—when we are taken up into his immortality, and into the love and unity of his body—it is then that we can say that heaven and earth are truly in the process of becoming one.

www.ingramcontent.com/pod-product-compliance
Lightning Source LLC
Chambersburg PA
CBHW020019050426
42450CB00005B/551